Homing

Homing

New & Selected Poems

Linda Rogers

Ekstasis Editions

Published in 2012 by:
Ekstasis Editions Canada Ltd.
Box 8474, Main Postal Outlet
Victoria, B.C. V8W 3S1

Ekstasis Editions
Box 571
Banff, Alberta T1L 1E3

LIBRARY AND ARCHIVES CANADA CATALOGUING IN PUBLICATION

Rogers, Linda, 1944-
    Homing : new & selected poems / Linda Rogers.

Poems.
ISBN 978-1-897430-83-5

    I. Title.

PS8585.O392H66 2012   C811'.54   C2012-901478-8

Ekstasis Editions acknowledges financial support for the publication of *Homing: New & Selected Poems* from the government of Canada through the Canada Council for the Arts.

Printed and bound in Canada.

For RVK

CONTENTS

Homing

Apocryphal Stories

DUST ADJUSTING

She buried the bird that hit her
window, and a day later the grave
moved. It could have been an
optical illusion or seismic event
followed by another dirt ruffle,
no sound, just dust adjusting its
place in the firmament. Then a
feather, then a wing. What could
she say? It wasn't sexual. She
thought of giving birth, or being
born, or dying - familiar flights
from darkness into the light - of
children, all of them afraid in the
dark, buried in earthquakes.

After the thunderstorm in Goreme,
(Can you believe it; she waited under
a tree for the rain to stop while the
wild horses of Capadocia flew off
with their electric dead?) the light
was like that, as if every tree and
rock were plugged in. O paradox!
La luce! When we mean too bright
to look at we say luminous, engaging
our adaptation for magical thinking.

Did the earth move then, shuffling
The cracked plates that rock the
cradle of civilization, swallowing a
child, breaking up the ice on Mount
Ararat and ancient cities where a
Sufi poet went to hear God in the
silence of snow. It wasn't sexual,
except in the ways everything is.

All she noticed was the peculiar
smell of ozone and supernatural
light. Remembering the bird that
rose out of her garden, one wing
at a time, she knew before anyone
else might have predicted that the
re-birthed infant emerging from
waters petrified into stone would
announce her name, Azra, meaning
pearl, mirror of the sea, and life
as we know it would begin again.

JOURNEY OF THREE

ACT ONE: THE WINDOW

She wakes up slowly, sees what
children see, life before colour.

The world in her window, frame
by frame, is pale; flickers of light
define the shapes as percussive
sounds become music. She rises
from her narcotic sleep. Light
gathers and articulates new words
for her spell: butterfly, bird, grass
and leaf. This is the time she's
been given to save the garden for
the ones she has given permission
to dress in the colours of praise.

It is morning, time for her morphine.
When her nurse releases the blind,
the shadows become real again.

ACT TWO: THE ONLY CHEMICAL THAT HELPS

This is the worst part. It is not death.
It is the oil slick of despair, when fear
is the only chemical keeping her alive.
There is little strength left in her. Soon
she'll be a nurse log rotting in the forest
sinking into the middle of Middle Earth.
This is her nightmare of slippery walls,
where hungry *rakshas* circle and howl.

There are no words for what they want
from her and what she won't give them.

I am afraid, she cries out to the wild
parameters of darkness, but soon she
will understand that she was glad to be
feeling something, anything in her
journey to the deep bedroom where
the dinosaurs sleep and decompose,
where her painful songs are liberated
in burps and bubbles of methane rising,
rapturing up to the roof of the world.

This might be night, but it is the season
when she adjusts her eyes to the light.

ACT THREE: BECOMING

This is the time when viscosity
spreads itself thin, when there
are holes in the dark, handholds
and footholds, no time to grieve
or look back. There is no vertigo
in heaven, or whatever hides itself
in the silent space between stars.

This is the time of acute hearing,
when she is beyond words but still
listening to the sound of her own
breathing, the sound of her mother
labouring, her blood pooling, the
holy water of what comes next
anointing all her articulate parts.

This is the ascent.

Now she knows she is giving birth
to herself, to a bird, an airplane, the
bride of the man upstairs, if he is a
man, if there is an upstairs, something
more than a factory freezing water
to confuse the people downstairs. This
is the lace of my being, she thinks
in pictures; I am becoming snow.

STORY OF TWO, THEN ONE

It's no different now than it was
when the gospel shoes were new.
Then they were magic, the shoes
of the fisherman walking on water,
the sandals of children who safely
crossed the desert at night & boots
dropped from airplanes with angels
inscribed on their leather soles.

Then we believed that the washing
of feet was an article of faith, that
the tongues in gospel shoes were
made to sing for our lady peace &
prophets spoke the truth because
their soles had immaculate wings.

Then we believed in miracles because
red poppies grew out of earth packed down
by soldiers who fell with their boots on.

Then we believed the story of two,
in genius, the dominant gene that
connected the I to the us. Au pairs!
The sound of crickets rubbing their
wings together, the tense vibrato of
mandolin strings. That was then &
now we pray for peace in the garden
at the end of the world, where foot
prints melt in the snow, and worn
gospel shoes keep perfect time - the
invisible, indivisible, music of one.

OUR HAPPY VOCATION

In the beginning, it's so gentle we
hardly notice. We are thrilled: by
the scent of jasmine and mulberry
leaves spun in the love extremities
of insects with happy vocations, by
those narcotic moments when the
silk tightens around our necks, and
the brain contracts like a womb.

There are so many guilty pleasures
for a witness addicted to language,
we sometimes forget the truth is a
song that is played on lethal strings.

We live for the frisson of male and
female words: naked bodies tumbling
in the corridor of bliss, sometimes
failing to notice poets with bruised
throats falling around us, their indelible
hands staining its paper walls.

We dip our fingers in the deeper wells.

In Tehran they came like water, a
green river of pilgrims, lassoing the
minarets with nooses of light. *O
Rubayat*, this is our happy vocation.
Sex and death are as simple as words
on a page, the reason we go there every
time a story asks to be told, every time
a prophet is blinded by angry gods.

APOCRYPHAL STORIES OF OOLONG AND GREEN

You might notice something is wrong; but
his world is perfect so long as the kettle boils.
"Tea is the cure for everything." He believes
in the sacrament of leaves steeped in water,
the apocryphal stories of oolong and green.
Every morning, it is something different.
He gets up at dawn to deliver his tea bags,
sometimes Darjeeling, sometimes Jasmine,
sometimes flavoured with citrus bergamia.

He has forgotten everything else. Think of
his skull as a cracked pot, mysteries steeping
inside. Is his first memory the sound of
the firmament breaking? Did his Creator
sit up in bed, enjoying a peri-natal cup,
three bent fingers tapping her saucer,
asking questions that can't be answered?
Or was it the thwack of his thin as porcelain
head bone landing on the hospital floor?

Why didn't somebody catch him?
Could he never get her attention,
even though he brought everything
there is to know about tea from a
previous incarnation, information
that never leaked out when what-
ever it was that broke got broken?

"You can use tea to wash your mirrors and windows,"
he announces because he wants to see Normal when
he looks in. What do we call Normal when our friend
brings us the news of the world every morning: from
India, China, Bangladesh, Malawi, Brazil, Japan
Russia and Tanzania, all of us sharing the same cup?

KINDLENACHT

Round midnight, the city's an open
book, every window a page framing
a story, men and women walking
through walls as the lights switch on,
reading real-books and Kindle, an old
word for birthing rabbits and fires that
burn widows and awkward truths.

Chapter One begins with the smell
of paper and ink, a child dreaming
his way to the end of a fairytale read
by a parent at bedtime, and a fast
talker, allergic to paper, texting into
her me-phone, Burn baby burn; and
soon the snarling bookends are out
on the street lighting matches while
the poet stands behind her lace curtain
watching a man with a camera take
pictures of rooms lined with kindling
bookshelves and sleepwalking kids
still asleep, fanning the flames.

Next the photographer snaps
poppies rising up from cracks in
the sidewalk, bringing advice from
the Old Town sleeping under the
pavement. Now it is time for the
poet with paper wings to decide.

She hides a dandelion deep in her
pocket, steps out on the windowsill,
exhales, makes a wish and jumps –
a new astonishment falling out of
the flames: a seed, a tree, paper,
the book that will say – now and
forever - wherever there is fire,
shadows will dance on the walls.

CRAWLING DOWN THE BEAUTIFUL

The rivers of Yugoslavia
are swollen with women
growling like the bellies of soldiers
who eat and drink too much
and take their post prandial naps
on the porch of the Hotel Sonia,
where comfort women are kept.

Picture the men with their mouths open,
leaning old wooden chairs against the wall,
their spurs digging into the floor.

If you were to hide in the top branches of a tree
strewn with the undergarments of martyrs
you would hear snoring and digesting,
shouting water, outraged girls full of spawn,
their bodies bruised by men and rocks,
and hungry wolves searching the riverbanks
where the victims abandon their shoes.

The rivers of Yugoslavia have
beautiful names; Drava, Morava,
Drina, words a man might say in
the dark, into the ear of his beloved,
the same man who carves his name
in the bellies of Bosnian women at
the Hotel Sonia. These women
remember the faces of the men
who cut and raped them, took them
out behind the Hotel Sonia and, good
Christian soldiers, hung their dresses
and undergarments, their loose teeth
like Christmas tinsel on trees,
then threw them into the river.

What you hear is not just water or water music
by famous composers. These women, Nadia,
Sophia, Mila, Oriana- swallowed by wolves like
the duck who cried Wolf! in the Russian fairytale,
are calling out the names of the men who drowned
them as they crawl down the beautiful rivers of
Yugosalvia, back to the ocean we came from.

from Heaven Cake

INVISIBLE NEIGHBOURS

Her husband only cried once as, one by
one, their invisible neighbours died: in
burning houses and fiery wrecks, once
a handful, Sam and Them, a collective
noun for invisible men, drank Gestetner
fluid stolen from the Residential School.

Every summer, it seemed, they buried a
child in the orchard. But he only wept
for the boat that burned when the barn
filled with new mown hay went up in
smoke. He'd loved that dinghy he made
from yellow cedar with the carved head
of a spawning salmon on the bow. The
soft wood was beautiful to work with.
It's as easy as cutting into butter, he'd
said; or killing someone with a word.

Their neighbour taught her how to carve
and make cedar root baskets. He told her
the beaver are territorial and had to fight
to the death. Nature is cruel, he said,
meaning all of us. Their neighbour taught
her to pray, not just for little children in
missions for whom she'd saved pennies
in Lenten boxes, but also for the men in
black who came with Bibles to save them.

When she sees all of them, her invisible
friend, her husband, the children standing
between the welcome figures carved from
yellow cedar, the visible human gate to
Spirit Square, their patina also golden,
she finally understands why her husband

had only wept for the trees that protect the
people who sleep in doorways, the children
who lay awake in dormitories, the ones
who drowned paddling logs away from
the residential school on Kuper Island,
and the fish struggling upriver to spawn,

All Our Relations.

THE GRASSHOPPERS' SILENCE

Listen to the story the prisoner's wife
hears in the Bengali darkness: the
one he'd told her about a grasshopper
he'd caught in his sweep net at dusk
and taken home in a glass jar with
breathing holes punched in the lid.

"Why do boys catch insects?" she'd asked,
and he'd answered: "Because they are lonely."

He told her the alarmed grasshopper
fiddled, rubbing its leg against its
belly. In Bangladesh, as in China,
ancient violins have one string; and
they sing in minor keys. "Why is their
music so sad?" she, asked him, even
though she already knew the answer.

"Their music is sad because grasshoppers are sad."

In Bangladesh, unfaithful women are
called "grasshoppers," because the
adulteress bugs jump from leaf to leaf
in monsoon swamps. "Don't ever leave
me," her husband had ordered his
captive insect, pulling off one of its
legs before he made it a suit of rags.

"Did it ever sing after that?" she'd asked.

His wife was a curious woman who'd
gazed past the Chittagong Hills to praise
the sunrise, its clamorous golds and
vermilions. "Don't *you* ever leave me,"
he'd said to her every time she opened

a book or looked out the window, her
eyes astonished as water lilies opening
to the first light of dawn. And that one
last time, "You left me," tearing out her
eyes and leaving them both alone in the
dark - her in a room without windows and
him in the prison he'd made for himself,
listening to the grasshoppers' silence.

THE PRECIOUS

The earth provides. It all came
out of the ground: a Frenchman's
skull, his teeth eroded in places
touched by his mother tongue,
& conflict diamonds traded for
weapons to put in the hands of
child soldiers in Sierra Leone.

The head is small. It could be
that of a child watching flies lay
eggs in the dead bodies of dogs
hit by cars & kicked to the curb,
or the incandescent loci of rogue
bullets singing in the jungle at
night. Maybe it is what it seems,
French bone shrunk in an English
speaking laundromat, and then
covered with costly fairy dust.

Will the jeweled skull fit in the
evening purse of an armaments
heiress, or will it hang in a disco,
its blood diamonds winking to
the beat of electronic music?

For the love of God, the woman
who pushed the artist's body into
the light cried out when he showed
her the precious head encrusted
with thousands of flawless gems,
what *are* you going to do next?

CLOSELY WATCHED TRAINS

The pianist wears green lace,
her skin showing in places.
In the first movement, we see the hunted
child, largo, framed in silent pictures,
between arabesques in an iron fence
around an old garden in Prague -
and later in the camp kindergarten,
lined up at the barbed wire with other
children thin enough to fit in the spaces
between notes by Beethoven,
played over a loudspeaker.

It is fifty years later.
She is alone at the keyboard now,
two hands for arguing voices, the sonata in D minor.
O Freunde, nicht diese Tone,
words by the poet Schiller for a deaf composer.
Nizkor, they say, remember she learned to play
what she heard on that barbed wire, her
starved wrists bridging dissonant notes.

At school, after the war,
we were given pencils to sharpen
and black-and-white
maps of Europe to fill in.
Some of my classmates remembered
passing on trains from colour to colour -
the names not red or pink,
but Hungary, Czechoslovakia, Poland.

O Freunde, nicht diese Tone.
"O friends," the phrase begins in strange arpeggios,
"not these sounds," the grace notes
sighing inside a sinister left hand
driving closely watched trains.

It isn't the sonata in D minor we're hearing
tonight, but the time between notes, when
children vanished through cracks in the earth.
At every rubato, we think her heart has stopped,
but then something moves in the green lace.
We see the child in the garden, spreading
foliage, her fingers remembering, the fence,
the music - something beautiful for God

from Love in the Rainforest

Miracles

MEND

Mend. She's heard the world a thousand times:
when the teacup shattered, when her fairy dress
tore on a nail, when she fell off the swing and
broke her arm. Mend it with kisses, her mother
said when she tripped on the sidewalk, using
the female word: M for Mother getting between
a child and sad outcomes. Mending. Everything
in her empirical world breaks or wears out: her
cat, her doll, and her crayons. These are her first
lessons in grief. On Christmas Eve, she saw a
family wearing antlers with lights ride through
a green light on a bicycle built for five. "Is that
him?" she asked. "It's *them*," her father answered.

To the next question, "Where are they going?"
he replied, "The end of the world," meaning
every-where on this night of magical thinking,
but she was afraid. All she'd heard him say was
"The end" Does the world end? On Boxing Day,
she takes that question to her closet with all
the Christmas ribbon and string and begins
her ball, which, over time, gets bigger and
bigger as she adds pipe cleaners, rubber bands,
anything that ties one to the other. She unravels
her favourite sweater, takes the laces out of her
shoes. She won't come out 'til it's done. There's
a knock on the door." What's going on in there,"
her mother wants to know? "I'm mending," she
shouts defiant, jubilant, all the emotions a girl
owns when she discovers she can make something
beautiful. When her mother orders, "Come out,"
she has to. She opens the door and rolls out
a ball as big as her world and both mother
and daughter have to believe she will fix it.

SHIVERING IN

Her feet are cold. The water is dirty.
Tricks, magic, alchemy, miracles –who
cares, so long as it works –the bitter
pills, the placebos, a child shivering in
shallow water, speaking in tongues.
Watch this daughter of Lysistrata make
the welcoming gesture. This is her movie.
She is the star and director of what comes
next. The tide will turn when Ta'kaiya
rotates her wrists and stops the action.

*Sorceress, bewitcher, diviner, prophet; she knows
her legends, the story of Raven who wrestled the light,
the psalmist who smote a giant with one small rock.*

He was a singer too, brought a king
to his knees with stories he told on a
fretless instrument. Lyre, liar; no one
tells the truth when sleeping dinosaurs
rise to the surface and turn the clean
water black. Only the child born with
a hole in her heart can change it - blood
pumping, oil pumping, water moving
over imperfections - using an old pair of
rosary pliers to fix the circle, transposing
the sacred music to a major key. Oh sad,
the hair that falls out, the fish that sicken
and die on the beach, the imperfect engine.
Is the child with special knowledge
singing for us or for them, the ones who
rise up from middle earth with fire in
their mouths swimming for their lives?
Can she make room for all her relations?

ADAGIO in G MINOR

It is almost always a miracle when
hungry people line up for bread and,
while the line moves slowly, adagio
in the language of music, angels tune
up their voices and the bread divides.

This was the sound in the sky when
the people of Sarajevo waited that
morning, their stomachs rumbling
as loud as gunfire in the marketplace.

We have a name for it, agoraphobia,
fear of the sky and the place where
fruit and vegetables are sold, and
sometimes women and children
lined up for bread are scattered
among the loaves and fishes and
baskets of oranges, their hands and
feet measured in pounds and ounces.

No wonder Smailovic, the cellist,
trembled as he dressed in his white
tie and tails, no wonder the Adagio
in G minor had so much vibrato.
For twenty-two days, for twenty-two
souls, and then for twenty-two months,
while the bombs fell around him,
Smailovic sat in the ruined onions
and potatoes, the smashed melons,
the ghosts of his neighbours, and
played, every note for someone who
died in the line-up for bread.

from The Saning

THE EARTH MOVES AND BRIGHT

Hold on, the mother sings to herself
In the rain, holding her infant child
above the floodwaters. Hold on,
the orphan who sleeps standing up
will not let go of her doll. For one
hundred and one days they've been
waiting for the toxic waters to release
the souls of their loved ones. For one
hundred and one days they've been
praying for the children left behind.

We are a prehensile species, holding onto our children:
mothers giving birth in trees, remembering the lessons
of our simian ancestors, mothers holding on through
earthquake, hurricane and plague, when the earth
moves and bright angels, their bones bleached white,
the colour of mourning, fall through the cracks.

Now, after one hundred and one days,
the trees are receiving the voices of
souls come back. Does water polluted
by death without blessings, *le dernier*
priye, release the voices of angels or devils?
Who is it that speaks when the wind of
savage gods whispers in leaves watered
by innocent blood? Do not question the
mothers and children with the world in their
hands, just praise them for holding on.

BONTEMPS

At dawn, nothing moves but the
sun rapturing up and up the way
yolks desire to slide back in their
shells and the desert shifts: indigo,
Murado, the delicate pink of orchids
and fresh heads crowning between
day and night. Could this be the
moment when everything happens?
Oh sweet! Let the good times roll.
On the asphalt highway from now
to never, a child with chalk writes
verses, the poems and prayers he
remembers from previous lives.
Begin the beguine. The orchestra
buried in sand plays *sotto voce*,
will not wake up the dead sleeping
peacefully or the living tapping
on underground walls with spoons.
Save me! Please save me! Wake up
the dinosaurs! Or not. We all fall
down and get up. Someone put a
sock in the hole in the ocean. The
garden has burped and the desert is
mine again, he writes, makes the
terrible scream of chalk on the road.

It could be human. It could be animal.
The desert is mined with explosives
and beautiful things he hid in his past
times: the orange blossoms preserved
in honey, the flavoured condoms, the
glass slippers. Who will sip, sip, sip?
Oh, his beautiful, beautiful things. The
child knows. He's heard it before. He

believes his family songlines, knows
every cactus has sweet water; and as
sure as his pavement chalk washes away,
he knows his desert will bloom again.

JARDI TANCAT

This is a dance we all know from the
time before rain, when birds pecked at
their breasts and drank blood, when
the only relief from the sun was stars
that blew out the lights in the night air
around them, when mothers taught their
children to pray and sang them to sleep.

In a room at the bottom of the world,
the miners wait for water and news of
their rescue, and their mothers, wives
sisters and daughters pray in the closed
garden, bang their heads on its invisible
walls. While a guitar weeps and the radio
woman sings in major keys, everyone
dances, birds with broken wings, women
planting hope in the driest desert on Earth,
while miners, buried alive, imprecate
stars that glow in the clear desert air to
light the tunnel that will bring them back.

You could say we all come from holes
in the ground, from mothers planted
upside down, their faces turned from
the unrelenting light, their nether ends
withering in thirsty air. The dancers are
thirsty. The miners are thirsty, sucking the
moisture from their socks. In the first
miracle of the branches, leaves sprouted
on the staffs carried by pilgrims lost in
the desert, who longed for the smell of
orange blossoms and the taste of oranges,
some so eager they ate them skin and
all when the sky relented and wept.

ESPERANZA

It took so long, so many hours
in the night for her fingers to form,
for her eyelashes to grow. Will she
remember what the waiting was like,
when she and her father shared a
mortal darkness; will they panic
in crowds? What was she thinking,
swimming in circles, navigating
the gyre in the days before light
when her mother's heart pumped
grief? Will she remember the tunnel,
her mother's body convulsing while
her eyes slowly adjusted to light, to
the sun bearing down on the Atacama
desert where no one dared to blink,
all of them watching a hole in the
ground the way her mother had
stared in the mirror over her bed
when her head emerged at last and
the world began to breathe again.

THE NEXT TWENTY YEARS

Our cousins are so busy copulating they
never learn to read, but chances are their
ancestors heard the prophet Moses read
the tenth commandment. To covet is venal
but "love thy neighbour" for ten seconds is
their randy social gospel. Ten seconds of
joy, then the sisters have time to go down
to the river; but not to pray or to swim.

The Bonobo have no rituals other than sex
and they've watched the river turn red
when their Congolese neighbours pick up
sticks and go with the flow. Instead they
drink the cool water, lie on their backs in
the sun and touch their swollen genitals.

I've seen you lie in naked in the winter sun
that comes through our window, your good
right hand hesitating over the zone, perhaps
grasping for notes or top bananas; you always
try to avoid the green ones, your ars musica.

Our lusty relatives didn't invent pleasure.
Our grandmothers taught our mothers and
Aunties, their gracile daughters, to understand
love is better than war: taught them how to
sleep in trees and never fall to the ground;
taught their leggy frugiverous sons to hang
from the branches and rub their nervous
tummies together; taught them to lie down
in prurient piles rather than fight over ripe
bananas. Is it possible our *pan sapien* Congo
cousins have the secret to peace on Earth?

PERCUSSIVE ON IVORY

It happened one day, all of a sudden,
a miracle. The child's fingers began to
move by themselves, up and down the
keys, treble and bass notes blending like
the birds and the bees, a fifth apart. They
say elephants grieve. Is this the sound
they make: left hand, right hand dancing
under the gallows, one keeping the melody
going, the other turning off the gas?

There was a time when she had to play
for her life, for the child who slept beside
her, practicing his scales on a piece of
wood, singing along. They made it a
game. Most of the children would die;
their fingers worn down to the bone.

Now the old lady's hands are so small,
her wedding ring rolls on her finger,
is percussive on keys that could be ivory
consonants shivering under the ground
at Theresienstadt. Music, she says, is her
God. Playing has saved her so many times:
the Chopin etudes, poetry, her prayer.

AFTER THE FLOOD

During the floods in Mozambique,
a woman gave birth in a tree. In places
like that, they say, miracles happen
every day. Is this why so many Africans
listen to priests with white faces who
tell them that condoms leak and that
it is a sin to let women sing in holy
choirs? If we had ignored the flooding
and civil wars, we might have said that
tropical Mozambique was the Paradise
where the tree of knowledge of good
and evil tempted Adam and Eve. We
might not have heard the lamentation
of slaves singing in the holds of English
ships or the weeping elephants who
mourned the slaughter of their loved
ones for ivory. Blinded by gold from
King Solomon's mines and the rich taste
of cocoa and cashews, we might not
have noticed the child soldiers armed
with toys that actually killed people.

It was a miracle when a street dog in Maputo
died in childbirth and her barren sister was
able to suckle her puppies and when the
child soldiers finally lay down their arms,
trading guns for sewing machines and bicycles.

While the tall Makua tribesmen dance
on stilts, artists of the Nucleo de Arte
make metal dogs out of guns. Deserts
destroyed by men bloom with iron trees
inhabited by steel birds in their nests.
Now, the Malawi god sits on a throne

made from guns. In Mozambique, they
say that scars, stronger than the skin that
grows beside them, are the connective tissue
of love and guns transformed into art. Now
the children who learned the macabre art
of war transform their wounds into bandages
for the wounded. There must still be time
for them to teach *us* the art of peace.

from Muscle Memory

WHEN THE HEART OVERFLOWS

In the reconciliation ceremonies, deserters from
The Lord's Army step on eggs because eggs are
silent. They cannot speak of what has passed
and what still happens every night, when terrified
Ugandan and Sudanese children cross the thirsty
savannahs to shelters, running to stay ahead
of soldiers who raid the camps for girls to rape
and infect and for boys, who never got to be
children, to conscript in the adult game of war.

When the heart overflows, the African proverb
says, *it comes out through the mouth.* They believe
the eggs will not speak of children with amputated
ears and tongues, with their eyes gouged out, who
hear no, see no, speak no evil. Eggs lack lips, and
so do the boys and girls with butchered mouths
who would tell their stories on pain of death.

Unless you call out, who will open the door?

In Uganda, before a thousand people died every
day in the camps, before thousands of children
marched morning and evening across the derelict
farmlands, families used their precious wood to
make dream coffins for their loved ones - for the
wish mariner a boat; for the sky traveler an airplane,
and for the girl who loved music, her own guitar.

Now grandmothers bury their children in the sacks
that bring aid. There is so little time to grieve for
them and for the child warriors and sex slaves who
come back from the forests to trade in their guns
for hoes and sewing machines. *The axe forgets,* they
say, *the tree remembers.* Now, where children once

sang African harmonies and left the footprints of
dancing in the dust, grandmothers watch the broken
eggs for the miracle the white-comers promised when
they brought their Bibles to Africa. Is their Orisha
about to speak? Does their God have lips after all?

from Muscle Memory

GOSPEL OF KINDNESS

When our parents talked about war or cancer,
they said "margins," the no man's land between
safe and sorry, and "border," the zone where
wars were waged and no one was safe. We
"duck and cover" children sucked our thumbs
and rubbed the satin borders on our blankets.

Fear made us do it.

Who wanted to go to places that nobody loved,
where death waited in cells as explosive as
land mines, where angels in airplanes dropped
mercy bundles of shoes, food, and artificial
arms and legs on the desert, while the angels
on the ground were busy healing the wounded?

"He has no boundaries," people who built
fences around their glass houses said about
the kids who dove into unknown waters and
coloured outside the lines, some of whom
grew up to bring the gospel of kindness to
children missing fingers and toes while armies
and viruses marched through the dark? Who
else would have the courage to polish the cruel
edges of broken glass and make them as safe
as blankets to comfort the children of war?

from Take Heart, a Médecins Sans Frontieres chapbook

Sweet Street Bee Tweet

THIS BOOK

The alchemist plans to stay for the night, gets
in beside you, straightens the sheets, *you, me:*
makes sure all your nouns and verbs agree,
takes out the wrinkles with old prescriptions,
give you your medicine. *Open up! Say Ahhh!*
This is magic, the arc of the narrative, sow's
ear transformed, your new silk purse, straw
into gold. Yes! He's a shape-changer. Yes!
She's a trickster. Now she is comedy. Now he's
tragedy, a man/woman radio show with music.
Ta dum ta dum. The beat goes on, transposing
notes the trees must dream when holy winds
sing in their branches. This is the music of
being and *letting it happen.* It's your life, your
elixir, but Simon keeps saying: do this do that.
Blow out the candle. Never! You refuse to plug
in books or electric blankets. They do not love
you. The alchemist makes you feel better,
smarter, more adorable. Yes, to this and
that. Yes, to the real alchemist, the stories in
his closet, his lotions and potions, ancient
remedies. He washes your feet with words
of wisdom, kisses your eyes good night, says

Yes, to the narrative tide moving in and out
with the moon. Oh moon that captures the light
fantastic on paper. *O magnificat,* pages smelling
like trees pressed flat, taking the ink. Oh, aren't
you glad you walked into this story, purest silk
made in ancient forests by worms that ate
the legend of mulberry leaves, 400 threads
to the inch, glad you took this book to bed?

O

In a world where   water is scarce,
we spend time in the   bathtub disturbing
the surface tension *d' l'eau* with O, the shape of
mouths surprised by love before they are cleaved in
hearts that drown in the bath as candles burn down &
the evening we live in goes dark. Nothing lasts forever,
we learned in the disappointment of children who
chase bubbles across the lawn. In the children's
game we play night after night, we make the
bubbles formed by touching fingertips,
heart shapes water never forgets,
the song of before, the
rhyme of again &
again.

SWEET STREET BEE TWEET

I be the queen bee in the garden of Guerrero, teacher man, street fighter, fighting war on poverty, war on mediocracy. His name Gueeeeerrrreeeerrrrrrroooo sounding like buzzzzzzzzz on slide guitars, sounding like new city of goddess, bee gardens rising out of Armageddon, sounding like bumblee bees buzzing, sounding like honey dripping, our choir: some singing high, some singing low, some fanning the hive ftftftftftftftftftft. Oh sweet, this garden of knowledge, me, queen bee showing the sweet life of bees to kids from the street. Ooooohhhh sweet the garden of Eden where children eat from the tree of good, no evil, apples falling close to the tree. Sweet, our garden surrounded by grundies drinking tea/ party with lemon, grundies with stings in their holsters tasering bees, tasering kids sucking honey from the hive, our *maison lumiere*, our paper house, walls singing poetry, singing equations, showing how honey equals infinity, the speed of light, moving fast as electric shocks, fast as speeding epithets - bees singing spells, bees singing the gospel according to bees. Sweeeet poetreeee. Singing bzzzzzzzzz zzzzzzzzzzzzzzzzzzzz thou shalt, thou shalt thou shalt thou shalt suck flowers in Guerrera's garden of good, thou shalt chew up paper and build beautiful hives, zzzzzzzzzzzzzzzzzzzz thou shalt imbibe the wisdom of paper. ABC 123 thou shalt spell like me, count like me, count like bees in our luminous cubicles, capsule hotels: queen bee licking, girl bees licking, boy bees licking, elixir of love, licking the hive healthy, licking the healthy hive, and the good news is: when the warrior dies, when the old queen dies, when the boybees die, when the girlbees die, so long as children lick honey, the garden will go on without us.

DZUNUQ·WA

You expect an old woman,
way past her stale date,
dragging her wrinkled
breasts on the sidewalk,
curdling her milk; but I'm
as new as the weeds that
grow through the cracks in
the pavement, the young
loons singing on artificial
lakes; and I will, yes, I do
keep coming back from my
time in the woods. Huuu
uuuuuuuuuu. I come with
the animals chased from the
forest. I come with my hunger,
my thirst for justice. I come
with my old friends, my new-
every-year body painted in
designer colours, Frog spit
on my breast, Susiutl slung
over my shoulders, Star on
my forehead, and always my
blood singing through. Uh-
hooooo. You can't resist my
lips by Revlon, mouth wide
open, ready to swallow side-
walks, streetlamps, hydroponic
children growing tame in the
garden you think you own.

from Framing the Garden

CUDDLING THE QUEEN

All over the world, bees are struggling
to maintain their hives; some of them
fanning, some of them sweeping, some
of them making love to old queens.
They shut their multiple eyes so they
don't have to witness death when their
needles stick in the groove. Ah! Ah!
What was once ecstatic piping is now
the sound of failure, jalopies failing to
start. We need new queens, some drones
shout above the sound of fanning and
flagellation as the damaged hives erupt.

"Cuddle the queens. Cuddle the queens,"
the hive jesters thump their tympanic
bees knees together. Who'll volunteer
to cluster and steal her breath? Tell them
they can still get away with murder in
this world of compound lenses. When
a few of the hive mates begin to move,
move it, others follow, pick up their sable
pens and brushes, un-fold their wings.

Cry matricide when the love children of
common mothers are brave enough
to dance in the cross-hairs of powerful
weapons, the failure of mercy. Cry down
with the old hives, dirty and dangerous.
Cry down with the old queens, drunk
on beeswax, the elixir of greed. Smoke
'em out. Rebuild the hive. Call it prayer.

BLOOMSDAY YES!

I let him suck one toe at a time when the children weren't looking 'til
YES! he got all worked up with the feet & the little footsteps creeping
back & forth getting tasty things from the kitchen Anatolian goat
cheese dripping pomegranate sauce rosy apples & fig pudding **OH!**
his face was pink his breath came quickly I waited and waited & finally
when the fire burned down I said **YES!** & covered my mouth while he
let out the air but not a sneeze it was sad and sneezing is *cumbus* the
Turkish word for joyful *cumbus* as hanging upside down like monkeys
'til somebody says soul come back his twenty one grams are escaping
and his lily's wilting was he going to deflate forever and ever was he
afraid of **YES!** was my **YES!** too filled with longing or could he hear
the grocery list in my cartoon bubble the food for our wedding the
cold salmon the provolone the amoretto cake the throwing rice the
case of champagne was he worried the soufflé would fall the cham-
pagne would go flat was the waiting better than the feast coming later
the wedding night maybe a cold fireplace a cold hotel room my feet
cold under the blanket me saying **YES!** but not meaning **YES!** just
thinking do we want to die in one another's arms how many days or
years from now both of us cold like this his spit on my toes turning to
ice while the world warms up & how could he know I'd make him rice
pudding & take him to dance class & make him tango in feet going
this way & that way me caressing his shins with my lovely dance shoes
the Spanish leather turning him on all the while thinking **YES!** so long
as the music plays **YES!** to the tango **YES!** to the nightgowns that
come in the mail the poor mailman weighed down with desire **YES!** to
kisses & cuddles **YES!** to the slice of moon with one star **YES!** to the
aphrodisiac bazaar the laquum pasha the love hotels the szaz at mid-
night the mandolin all night long yes to the comb the falsetto singing
YES! to the hearts on my toes & the toe sucking his toe in the door
come in **YES!** to his Theremin cracking the firmament **YES!** to the
earth moving **Yes!** Please.

EARTH MOVES

It's amazing how some species manage
to have sex in the air or in water, or
up a tree where the agonized mating
songs of raccoons rattle branch and
root, disturbing the dirt. Earth moves
and old neighbourhoods shift. When
the first continent (fragile home of
the insatiable Bonobos) exploded, our
dolphin ancestors swam through the
cracks, their genetic memory songs of
sea mammals steering the diaspora.

When did it begin, the congress between women
and silkies, sailors and singing mermaids, sirens and
warriors becalmed on the return voyage from Asia
Minor, and ghosts haunting the floating city?

Whose voices break in the tangle
of Japanese villages floating across
the Pacific Ocean to world without
end waiting on the beaches near
Mile Zero and Boonville, California,
where hog rings and mouse ears
line up for inter-special moments,
cell-division in the new millennium?

We are mostly water. Will mutants
surviving death and the little death,
born in the sludge of disaster, shed
their dissonant scales on beaches with
rusty landmines and guns pointed across
the sea, whisper their tragic provenance
to girls who laugh at the breast-shaped
moon and bed them down in the sand?

Fairy Tales

THE PIGEONS

Was the egg in the nursery rhyme just a
child when the secret police pushed him
into the cosmic crease? It's an old story.
This time, he is Hamza Ali Al-Khateeb,
named for prophet's uncle, who died in
battle, one moment on the wall and the
next falling into the catalogue of grief.

Is this what we mean by invisible borders,
world cracked open, each half a mixing
bowl; infant skulls cracked on the sides?

So long as battery mothers breed in cages
designed by Strangelove; so long as they
lay eggs with spots of blood in the yolks,
he will mix the ingredients for hell bread –
dispensable gingerbread boys sent out to
stop red trajectories, some of them small
enough to fit through the eyes in sweatshop
needles. some flying higher than the
pigeons tumbling over Syrian villages.

What do we say when we see yolks falling
through time, whipped into trembling: could
be sunset, could be thermonuclear fireworks,
spectacular Armageddon, infants diving like
stickmen from windows in the land of Oz?

They say the brain is layers of whipped
meringue and the head bone is fragile
as eggshell, the colour we paint interior
rooms invaded by madmen given access
to sleeping children. Who gave the demon
permission to stir in the names of boys

like gentle Hamza, who raised the pigeons
that carried his prayers from mosque
to mosque; who must have looked up at
the sky crashing down on him and wondered
if Allah were only a large bird of prey sent
out to swallow all the innocent messengers?

HALO SHE SAYS

Don't go down, the bluesman sings
in a weary voice, *to Fannin Street*
while the wise child in the back seat
claps her hands to the music and
says *bye, bye* to the rear view mirror,
since she knows she's the one who's
moving forward. *You'll be lost and never
found. You can never turn around.*

We've come to the stop light. The music
stops and the radio tells us the world
is convulsing. Wise child knows more
than she can say, words like war, flood,
earthquake, and volcanic eruption.
She understands. I turn off the news
and return to the song, *I wished I'd
listened to the words you said,* startling
the punk kid at the bus stop who looks
up from his book and raises his hand,
two fingers, just as the sun jumps out
of a cloud and lights up his Mohawk.
Halo, she says as the light turns green.

TILLICUM

At residential school, the children
joined hands under the table and they
whispered, "All my relations" while
Father said grace. In the dark, before
he came to choose, they planned
their freedom rides across the water.

Some said it was better to find logs
on the beach and paddle with tree
branches. Others said they would wait
for the whales. "We'll catch a ride with
Tillicum," meaning "our brother" in
the Chinook language, the children
said when Father wasn't looking.

Several children disappeared on the
exodus from Kuper Island. When the
Orcas sang, I wondered if they were
trying to tell us what happened to
children and whales in captivity.

We say the same thing about captured
whales & stolen children as we do of
women in labour, "They will forget the
pain," but do they, their loneliness
breaching in every leap from the deep
pools where they grieve for freedom &
all their relations? Do we stop to think
that the Orca Tillicum, companion of
three drowned souls, might also be
desperate to find his way home?

NOTHING BUT YOUR BEAUTIFUL

There are words for this. You might
think I am casting a spell on you. Is
it normal to ask a boy for pieces of
himself to knit in a scarf - his hair
and fingernails? I've been saving the
things you left around before you
went on your wandering time – the
museum of you - a band-aid, a sock,
a roach, a pencil sketch, your tube
pass. I added chain for the ones you
are breaking. Isn't it crazy? We're
losing you anyway, the child we knew.

*This morning, before dawn, the time when
I see you upside down in the pond, your
hair disappearing like ink, I took the lid
off the cloisonné bowl where I keep your
milk teeth in a nest of baby hair and the
room lit up. Where did you find so much
light to bring into this troubled world?*

I have to confess I once knit a scarf
to protect a friend who wandered
into the cosmos and fell. I am telling
you this because grief's cold fingers
are gripping my throat again. You
might ask why I am knitting another
after all these years? It is because you
were seen walking in the rain wearing
nothing but your beautiful hair and
your laugh like running water? This
time I will not finish the scarf. So long
as I keep knitting, you will be safe.

GILASI

I am Gilasi, glass in Kiswahili, given
my name because light passes through
me. Some call me *zero zero*, ugly albino,
but mostly I am invisible, especially
now since the night the body-robbers
came with machetes and cut off my legs.

Now, I sit on the dirt floor waiting for
sleep that never comes. This is my time
for magical thinking. In my dream, I am
neither crippled nor blind. I am glass,
the window of myself opening so wide
I am free to fly to treetops and behold the
down from down, a place where I can look
up and imagine the weight of being that
leaves my body every time I sneeze or die.

This is when I watch myself circle the
world, a star transmitting broken light and
the sound of lamentation in zeros that signal
alarm to human and animal babies recreated for
defenestration, their radio heads heavy with
history, terrible falls in every incarnation.

*I am here to warn my babies that glass
is fragile and men with cruel machetes
will trade their infant bodies for money.*

My flying *Zuri*, beautiful children, stop to
eat the treetops' tender leaves. They taste
the sweet milk when panics of baby gazelles
and zebras, kicking up dust, stampede in the
Serengeti, arriving at the *Simba Koppe* by
sunset, in time to drink from the breasts of

new mothers adapting to every mutation.
The *mediwa,* beloved gazelles and zebras,
infants who *are* and are becoming as they
go round the sun and melt and change, we
hope for the better, don't need legs for that.

THE PERFECT DOOR

Wise child was born with an aura
blue as the ring around the moon,
made for special thinking and,
lucky rabbit, soft as the fur in hats
that pass through wedding rings.

He was born singing Three Little Birds,
the song on the cosmic telephone.
Don't worry about a thing/'cause
every little thing is gonna be alright

Imagine the boy with the light
bulb in his brain going up to the
big front door of the glass city,
seeing all the kids inside eating
candy from the tree of knowledge
and finding his key didn't fit.

Imagine him hearing the inside
voices, false teacher cries of lazy
and stupid, plugging his ears and
singing his rasta song, wiping his
feet on the doormat, a stop sign
he'd read backwards. Picture him
waiting for standing babas to pass
the plate of forgetfulness, his head
spinning like holy dervishes, body
thinner and thinner, and hopefully
someday small enough to slide
through the keyhole, waiting
for a real teacher to come and
guide him to the perfect door.

PERMANENT STAIN

She never found out why he stood
there night after night, blocking
the light from the hall. My door,
she couldn't quite say, get out of
my door, because he was gifted
with words, maybe not better than
she was, but his was all the power
and the glory - his name on the
deed, his bread on the table. Bread
of angels, he'd say, tossing off crumbs
of broken wisdom, the sacramental
wine long gone, down to the dregs,
elixir of *veritas* down the hatch.

He woke her from a dream that tasted
purple, the colour of bruised eyelids, the
permanent stain on the grape crushers' feet.

It's almost always too late to ask
men like him what or who robbed
their joy, what deafening slap to
the side of the head, which copped
feel in the locker room, which
friend blown up in war or dragged
down the highway, nothing but
tire marks left on his flesh. By the
time she stopped to think and ask,
he'd slowly erased himself from
the shadows that never got folded
up and put away in the drawer of
forgetting. This might be why she
shook him after he died, shook him
hard, asked him why when the gift
of the gab had left him so soon.

CRI MAMA

It's nap time. Her grandfather plays her
favourite tune, "Voodoo Queen Marie,"
on his mandolin and she dances until
she falls asleep, curled up with her
thumb in her mouth. This is how we
found her great-great grandfather the
afternoon he died, one hundred years
after a distant ancestor's spirit departed
his cracked skull when a rock hit him
during a slave revolt in Santa Domingo.

While she sleeps with her dolls, a
reporter drops his camera and runs to
pick up a child with a head wound
lying in the ruins of Port au Prince.
This baby is a lifeless doll among
dolls. We do not know if she's quick
or dead, but he's found her curled
up with her thumb in her mouth on
the street where the dead sleep with
the living and zombies wait for rocks
to move the way they did for *Mon
Dieu* in the Garden of Gethsemane.

*Did we hear two girls calling in unison
when our granddaughter cried, "Mama!"
in the middle of a very bad dream?*

It is hard to imagine the fathers of far
apart sisters asking their mothers at the
moment of conception, "Did the earth
move?" Yes, it did, both times. Now
their world has shifted, opened up and

revealed *vu deux,* both sides, the back-
stories of girls with Creole blood with the
same Latin root, *Creare,* meaning to be
born or reborn, both calling "Mama"
from opposite sides of the hemisphere.

SILVER FOIL

A match strikes in the dark
and another silver paper
floats to the ground in
cities where lost children lie
in the same direction as snow.

A woman who gathers them up
every morning and sells them to
tourists says they are sacred relics.
Burn marks on the foil could be
nails from the Garden of Gethsemane,
where white flowers with opium
seeds grow out of the bodies of men.

She believes they are beautiful
just as the lost children living on
sidewalks all over the world
believe a sky full of babies in
pale dresses could land, just
once, with a prayer on them.

This is how the sky falls down
on quiet streets in London, Paris,
Havana and the Barrio Gotico in
Barcelona, where snow has the
sound of mercy and stoned children
come out of the shadows, take off
their gloves and wait for angels
with trumpets and small feet to march
across their outstretched hands.

The woman who collects the silver
foil and trades them for food for
the hungry calls them her veil of
tears when the solstice moon
blossoms in poppy fields and small
addicts with their arms held out,
chasing the dragon, stand still as
crosses in the middle of the road.

from The Saning

THE ETYMOLOGY OF FREEDOM

"Stars," the infant says, looking up.
She can almost hold this small
constellation in her hands – libra,
the seventh sign, balanced between
virgo and scorpio. She lives in a
house without walls, stacks of books
that reach from here to never, the sky
open, revealing the biggest screen
ever imagined, a portal for every
pixel of wisdom curious children
discover in the binary universe.

She stands on the edge of the world, her feet in the ocean
that divides continents, and, in every city and village on
this side of the mountain high enough, the valley low enough,
the river wide enough, the world is her library, a word made
available when bark first peeled off the tree of knowledge.

On the far side of the world, other
children reach for the same stars,
repeating their own words, *seba*, in
Egyptian, *setareh* in Farsi. The sky is
their limit, even when the ancient
street of book-sellers runs with blood,
even when the library at Alexandria
burns again. The words for love and
liberty, bound at their roots, most
beautifully in *kindertotenlieder*, songs
for the love of children drawn to justice,
the small arrangement of stars in the
Southern Hemisphere, remain as
steadfast as the fire that gives us the
words that define civilization: library,
liberty, enlightenment, libido. These

are the lights that can't be turned off,
morning or evening on both sides of
the world. In rooms without ceilings
and walls made of bark peeled from
trees in the Rainforest and Elsewhere,
it is their human right to learn that
the etymology of freedom is reaching
up to touch stars that never burn out.

DOWN FROM THE TREE OF KNOWLEDGE

Does anyone remember when the first cell
divided? Was there grief at the seam that
slowly unraveled, when one became two?
Is the beginning of love or civilization
the moment protoplasm tears down the
middle, or what we call the little death?

Some hemorrhages are so small as to
be invisible to the naked eye, but even
small plants scream when their tiny
root systems are torn from the earth.

I gave my husband a pear from our tree
to eat. The fruit was warm and juicy,
perfectly symmetrical. By *pear* did the
inventors of language actually mean *pair,*
or two by two, the way Noah herded
animals into his wooden boat before the
flood, or pairing, the act of carnal love?

Is it true that we are mostly water and love
has a symmetry as fragile as wobbly molecules?

From time to time, the ocean tears itself
apart. It makes a sound like grief, or men and
women moaning during *le petit mort,* or
mothers pushing their young into the world.
Have we forgotten that? When the wave
full of boats and faces and little shoes comes
crashing onto the beach with the force of
cosmic orgasm, do we not already know the
sound a mother will make when she must
decide which of her children she will save?
What of the one she releases the way a tree

relinquishes fruit? Will that child ride the wave
singing, grateful for freedom, across the Pacific
to the beach at Mile Zero or will he drown
in sorrow? Will the mother comb the sand
each morning, searching for his little shoe,
or will she look away when she sees him
come down from the tree of knowledge
knowing his mother chose to let him go.

from Muscle Memory

THE BLUE DRESS

On the Poya, or full moon day, the photographer
took his parents to a shrine by the sea to pray,
as was their custom. The beach was crowded with
tourists, some of them Buddhist, some of them
sun worshippers lying in bronzed rows on the sand.
On the first drive by, he saw wire fences surrounding
rich peoples' gardens, and beggars who would have
been tempted by the papayas in their trees and silks
blowing on their clotheslines. On the second drive by,
he noticed a blue dress hanging from one of the fences.

He watched as the first waves brought fish to the shore
and saw laughing children run home with the catch in
their hands. It was a miracle. On the *Poya,* or full moon
day like the ones when Lord Buddha was born, attained
enlightenment and died, the earth moved and the ocean
delivered food to the hungry. When he stood on his car
to take pictures, he saw shirts hanging like prayer flags
on many fences to celebrate this holy time of reflection.

A few frames later, he saw the pale sunbathers tossed at
the high tide line. When the floodwaters carried him and
his camera down the road past the rich people's houses, he
realized the shirts & dresses hanging on fences were not
laundry or flags or dolls woven among the barbed wire.
They were arms and legs and faces strained from the angry
floodwaters the way whales capture fish in their teeth.
The little blue dress was a child who may or may not have
been playing in an enclosed garden. What does it matter now
which side of the fence he was on when the big wave struck?

from Muscle Memory

WEEP FOR AFRICA

In the last moment before sleep, when Darfura
closes her weary eyes and sees her grandchildren
through compound lenses, she thinks of herself
as a dog with row upon row of wrinkled teats.

Not so long ago, a bitch from a nearby village
brought a baby home from the bush where her
mother had left her to die. Lucky baby; the
recently bereaved animal nursed her. Darfura's
family watched, their eyes large, their tongues
swollen with thirst. Long ago, in the mission
school, she had written the word Dog on her
chalkboard when the nun asked for God. If God
were visible, a dog with access to the deeper
well, then how many nipples would she have?

In the dark, she remembers the taste of Jebel Marrah
oranges; how the children ate them skin and all.

She sees God as a fountain spraying milk in the
mouths of babies, spraying water on her dry
rows of corn, spraying the elixir of love on child
soldiers. In this season of flood and drought, she
is an old woman, almost forty. Her teeth are gone,
her empty breasts swing when she walks with her
hollow gourd on her head. She thinks they almost
touch the ground. That's where she's headed now-
to the ground where her children sleep alone, no
longer afraid of the darkness that brings children
with guns, no longer afraid of the love that kills.

from Muscle Memory

THE AMAZING COLOUR OF LUCKY

His daughter remembers Cuba, the night
he danced with her in the ballroom
of that grand hotel at the beach,
while the Caribbean sun dropped
through an evening the amazing
colour of oranges and lucky
amethysts in the bracelet her mother
gave him the day the baby came out of
the salt water sea between her legs.

In the Age of Aquarius, when it seemed
as if all the heroes were found
floating in turquoise swimming pools,
the pockets in their white summer
suits filling up with water, someone
wrote a song with the famous last
words that said when you're a junkie
the sun is always setting.

His daughter remembers latino music,
the Spanish guitars and the drums,
holding on to the waist of his tropical
suit for dear life, when her party shoes,
a size too big because her feet were
growing, kept slipping off and finally
danced by themselves on the hardwood floor.

He picked her up, held her suspended
the way I once saw a child held over
the ancient stairs in a sea wall, its
stones worn down by his ancestors
and the ocean, and said now you are
ready to swim, because swimming
is one thing you never forget.

His daughter's bare feet dangled over the dance
floor in the grand hotel in Cuba and she buried her
face in his neck, which smelled of salt and cigars.

When the sun fell into the ocean
and the electricity failed, as it does
every night in Cuba, she said she could
still find him on that dance floor the way
lambs in pastures find their mothers.
She smelled his white summer suit
with its pockets filling up with turquoise
water he was already taking on.

I have seen children move objects
just by staring hard at them. Maybe
she was sitting on the beach in front of
her house with the tree growing through
it, holding on to his white summer suit
for dear life, staring at the sun, willing
it there the evening we chased it down
the street where he was drowning in a
room with orange and amethyst windows,
a shotgun with one bullet in his mouth.

from The Saning

THE LAST PICTURE

It is hot in church. Sweat gathers in
their groins and armpits, creeps down
their spines as they attempt to keep
their minds on Holy Communion.

After they sing the last beatitude and
genuflect to the Holy Child, the lovers
rush home and put on their bathing suits,
make a quick picnic: a slab of provolone,
some pears and grapes, bread and wine,
then hurry to Torregavela Beach, where
the Roma children often swim naked.

While they rub one another's backs with
olive oil, two gypsy girls who've been
selling trinkets to tourists approach a
family building sandcastles. *"Insetto!"*
the mother hisses, collecting her children
and shooing the filthy Roma away.

The shooter catches Mother with her
mouth open so wide insects could fly in.
He snaps the Roma girls shrugging off
their dresses and running into the surf,
their hands rising desperately out of the
water which spits them back out in the
single moment between now and never.

The lovers are hungry. They eat their
picnic and think about *later.* Later, they
hope, they will make a child. They don't
even notice when the man with the camera
takes their picture. And they don't appear
to see the Roma girls laid out on the beach

beside them, their lifeless bodies covered
with towels. They keep on kissing and
feeding one another grapes, ignoring
the stunned photographer, who now
has a photo that will shock the world.

from Muscle Memory

THE SIGN

I found it after she left, the sign
and bold chalk marks, a linear
path through the garden, her left
brain in control, as if the birds
and the bees always fly in straight
lines from here to where. The sign,
also written in chalk, says *Grama St.*
the movie that plays in her other
mind: a magic narrative, the fairy
house, the brass bell that warns the
invisibles, living walls, some hybrid
roses, bonzai plums, wisteria, tiny
chairs, the china tea set, opium
poppies and day lilies, the wrought
iron fence she can play with a spoon,
the monkey bars in the park. One
rain, one careless move will erase the
letters. The storyteller will vanish.
Will she remember the words?

Brushes with Fame

THEREMIN TREMBLES

They called it miscegenation, but
Theremin never touched his bride,
only the air around her, the electrical
fields, adjusting volume and pitch,
channeling the voices of angels
wrenched from their life on Earth.

His ballerina trembled, possessed by souls
that rose up singing from the deeper well.

Were their names, husband and
wife, connected to Zombie tribes
that migrate from body to spirit,
written in invisible ink? No one knew
what had happened when Theremin
fell through a crack in the world,
maybe to his death, maybe to a
Siberian gulag; or when his bride was
seduced by the good vibrations in a
plantain garden in Haiti, the dress
rehearsal for what happened later,
when the Great Tremble swallowed
the city of Port au Prince and swept
the sleeping lovers in Petit Paradis
out to sea. And every time the question
is asked, why do men and women
step on cracks in the sidewalk, the
Ouija board answers, because when
the earth moves, they have to follow.

JAZZ REVELLATOR

In this *hamam*, there are only
stars in the ceiling, and the earth
bound angels who debride our
skin are naked. On the street,
they cover their faces; so no one
can see they are thinking of hot
summer nights when they lift
their veils to eat the *Ciya* fig
pudding that tastes of goats
grazing in mountain meadows
and the earth in paradise, then
and now an enclosed garden.

Do these women know that *Figa*
in Italian means the veil that covers
the garden of earthly delights?

Later, a jazz man singing praise for
his wife watches their bodies move
to rhythms as old as the sacred
music that once filled the domes
in the church of holy wisdom,
named for the saint whose
angel choir was covered with
plaster when the Ottoman
princes conquered Byzantium.

The veiled women don't know
the words written by slaves,
but they do understand that,
note after note, the plaster falls
soft as Pamuk's snow from
the faces of the seraphim with
six wings who undress in the

darkness at the Hagia Sophia
while the jazz man whistles
happy birthday to the woman
he loves, one note less every
year until the only praise left
will be the holy silence of wings.

PRAISE HIM, MORNING STAR, ST. LUCIA, LIGHT OF MY EYES

After Panagea blew up, the blind
poet swam here and there for almost
two millennia, following the dolphin
diaspora; found himself rowing a
wooden horse in the rosy fingered
dawn, and one day a sailing ship with
human cargo dragging its mournful
wake from Africa to Saint Lucia, her
bright white-candled crown burning
between two volcanoes. *Dove e la luce,*
he asks, the entitlement of blood that
flowed from Homer and Dante into the
warm current that carried him home.

Omeros sits under a poinciana remembering
the waves that rhymed on the first beaches, the
ivories keening, percussive elephant grief, while
he watches a colonial bride weave strands of
hair strong as the ropes that debride the hands
of men breathing hemp dust while they braid the
one consanguine strand in Her Majesty's sheets.

Omeros is drinking piton, volcano spit,
listening to lava warming up the smell
of rotting bananas, sweetsop and papaya,
listening to the gecko and parrot *aubades,*
listening to the ho-humming Irish bride,
wearing an orchid, one of her husband's
musk-smelling testicles, in her hair, twisting
corn silk tourist braids in the market, her
received accent as real as French ivory,
mother of toilet seats banging in posh
resorts. Oh, God bless the lovely Creole
bottoms. This girl has walked on water,

across the Aegean Sea and the Irish Sea,
right across the wild Atlantic Ocean,
her Jesus cross tied around her neck.

From time to time, the wife fingers her
love wounded girl/boy orisha, sniffs
her hands smelling like silk thread,
tourist hair, spices: ginger, cinnamon,
nutmeg, yellow peppers, and the gun-
powder scent of the seafaring man who
touches her when and if he comes home.

Her tourist stands perfectly still. Purring.
She must feel like a kitten, must love the
stroking; the Redcoat bride, Antilles pearl,
layers of beautiful sadness, twisting her hair,
which is long and slippery and straight.

Click, the gecko eyelids open and shut.

Omeros, the blind poet, takes pictures.
There is so much light, he doesn't need
a flash or even a camera. I'll soon be
immortal; the tourist thinks her way to
becoming a statue. She's on the radio,
riding the invisible polyglot wire from
Grand to Petit Piton, riding home to the
three part legend of herself, to Omeros.
She knows, when their braids are undone
she and the bride who weaves and unweaves
will hold these waves forever and ever, for
all their relations. Back to before these girls
ever beamed out of the ocean is something
only the blind poet is privileged to see.

THE WILDERNESS OF WRONG

Every Friday night, at the hour when
their countrymen sit down to family
dinners the *shabbas* candles lit but
never blown out for fear of bad luck,
mothers and fathers meet to pray for
peace at Sheikh Jarrah while their
children bear arms all along the walls
and fences that divide their people.
This is the Jerusalem hill where the
Jewish writer who refused to shake
hands with Israeli politicians embraces
his Arab neighbours. He has the
yafeh nefesh, beautiful soul that
some bigots describe as a bleeding
heart. This is where his pen draws
ink to trace the map of a land no
one owns. His is no country for men
and women who wander in the
wilderness of wrong thinking with
weapons that kill. It belongs to the
resilient plants, hawthorn and
terebinth, that feed on the blood
of boys like his son who died in
the Galilee Hills for no reason at all.

RED EYE FLIGHT

Inshallah, the gentle dervish
whispers and kisses both
shoulders as I step off father
mountain into a real lightness
of being. Was it this easy when
Lucifer fell out of heaven, his
angel mind in a twist? Did
the sky bleed when he fell?

Beneath, the Aegean turns red.
The Mediterranean turns red.
The sun is setting where
ancient lovers meet in rose
gardens under the sea,
their teeth stained with the
aphrodisiac pomegranate juice,
the bloodshed all forgotten.

Dido, Aeneas, Helen, Paris,
the power hungry Anthony
and Cleopatra, who had her
sister murdered in the temple
at Ephesus, all are forgiven.

Red is the new colour of love;
and I must be wearing rose-
coloured glasses. Am I falling
or flying like the hens that were
fitted with red contact lenses
when the cannibal flock began
pecking one other to death?

Feribots sail back and forth
between the ancient ports of
Smyrna and Haifa. Back to the
future, the *Mavi Marmara,* where
we sat on wooden benches and
drank tea on the passenger deck,
is washed with water as red as
the wake of whaling ships. If we
were all to wear rose-coloured
glasses, would the killing stop?

HER SEWING STONE

Who knows where her oval stone
came from. It could be a dinosaur
crystal, the third eye of Buddha,
a fragment of star, or the cold heart
of a glacier. It fits in his hand the way
a man fits a woman, perfectly; not
just any stone, but one that picks up
radio signals and sings in water, just
when he's forming the letters, *I am;*
just in time, but not soon enough to

sign his name beside hers the way she's
been practicing over and over. We know,
because there it is printed backwards on
her blotter, the letters formed the way they
would be if they'd taken turns holding the
oval stone, and he was guiding her pen, or

she was sewing her wedding dress,
the oval stone cool in her hand.

She has passed it to him and this is
how well it fits. Imagine a man with
a fever and a girl who has taken off
her clothes and run into a storm, then
comes back to his bed like that, her
nipples hard, her skin a frozen pond.
See how they fit like blades in ice, the
words coming easily. Their love is a
simple exchange of body heat, his
fever shaping notions of truth and

beauty as ephemeral as ice that sits
on his tongue and melts – the silence
of snow. Never mind the praise, or
bodies that fit for as long as it takes
to write a poem. Of them all – stone,
snow, love - only the words will last.

THE THORNBIRD

Every boy wants to go up on the
roof and fly. Some of them are
actually foolish enough to do it.
They tie capes around their thin
shoulders and wait for a divine
breath to lift them and take them
away. Where is it these boys who
fear women more than they fear
flying lessons are wanting to go?

*Some of them believe that death
means martyrdom. These dare-
devils hope for wings, but the air is
for birds and the dead who have
walked in kindness on the earth.*

When there is no wind, the boys
play with their guns. They aim
at singing birds, imagining they
have the power to stop the sound
of freedom and flight. Sometimes
they shoot girls, aiming at the heart
because they are afraid of love.

At the corner of Khosavi and Salehi
Streets in Tehran the *Basij* shooter,
a boy in a coward's cape, aimed
at the ancient heart of Persia, its
poetry and music - at Neda, the
song of her people. What the fool
didn't know is that you can't kill
a song. *Natarsid.* Neda may lie still,
but she still sings like the bird with
a thorn in its heart; her voice the

voice of millions led by her music teacher. *Natarsid. Natarsid. Mah hamed bah ham hastim.* Courage. Courage. We are all together.

SNAIL LOVE WITH OPERA

I think of you lying in jail at night
listening to the music you asked us to send,
thinking of her, while Beethoven's only opera,
Fidelio, the heartsick husband in prison,
plays in my head, and snails with soprano
voices make noisy love in our garden.

This is what Mozart meant when he wrote
Eine kleine Nachtmusik, A Little Night Music,
arias sung in flowerbeds, where slippery
inamorata, floating on silent carpets of dew,
make their slow way through the tea roses
and dahlias, forget-me-nots, to dirt
hotels where they twist and twist,
the pyrotechnic friction of flesh
making the holy madrigals of men
and women in love, just like you, all
alone, listening to music in your cell.

Was it Mozart who first called the love
portal of women a theatre? Was he
thinking of Venice, the first opera house,
and snails crawling out of the sea with
prisons on their backs, then filling
them up with air, the volatile mother
of water and music and the viscous
fluids exchanged when *camerata*, the
passionate stories, are sung in gardens
where luminous footprints of snails are
songlines people of genius are compelled
to transpose when the time on the ceiling
is almost dawn, and even the deaf
composer, lonely as the celibate tenor,
his candle burnt down to the wick,

only one song playing itself over and
over outside his window at night, is
able to free his hero Fidelio from the
agony of love with treble notes so high
and pure they can bend prison bars?

This is the sound of hermaphrodites
glowing in the dark, their bodies
acquiescing to the music of grass
harps and insect singing, their lyrics
produced from shining orifices in the face,
their opera houses lit up and the Midnight
Express freeing the prisoners of love,
all of them lying awake and listening,
so long as light shines through bars.

from The Bursting Test

LETTER FROM BOLIVIA

Every night now, Manuel rides
his bicycle the shortest way home
from Holguin University, his legs
pumping furiously because there
might be a letter from his son,
who is in Bolivia healing men
and women who were blinded
when Lucifer fell into the jungle.
Every circle of the wheel, Manuel
chants *"Seremos como el Che"*
because he is afraid for his gentle
boy who paints mariposas and
butterflies in his free time. Manuel
thinks he hears drums, but it's only
his father's heart beating in his ears.
There is still danger in the trees
where the martyr gave up his life.
Bad things have been happening
to the rainforests and the mountain
people it shelters, who, blinded by
light, run from tree to tree, feeling
their way to the clinics where Cuban
doctors operate to restore their sight.

It is forty years since the gun-shots
that killed San Ernesto de la Higuera
scared away the birds. We hear only the
keening of leaves in the clearing where
one lucky soldier drew a short straw
and the honour of pulling the trigger,

where the junta doctor cut off the dead hero's hands.

Manuel's fingers shake as he unfolds
his letter. He is overjoyed that his son
is safe. Today, Victor wrote, we gave
an old man back his sight. His daughter
sent a letter to the newspaper, offering
to kiss our hands, which had her father's
blood on them. It is a miracle, she said,
the way love heals. My father, Mario
Teran, whose vision you saved, was
the one chosen to shoot Che Guevara.

SHOPPING FOR REGLA

On Saturday morning, Regla
walks the streets of la *Habana Vieja*
dressed like an African Queen in gold
jewellery, high heels and spandex,
while her Santera aunties parade
in immaculate white, and bakers with
wagons push their trembling loads of
Sabbath cake through the tourist traffic.

All the ladies are beautiful, even the
aunties, who also make love to our lens.
The voodoo rule is tourists are allowed to
take one picture for one Yankee dollar.

Our cameras, exposed to the tropical
splendour of women with the exquisite
Spanish posture for dancing, shudder
when they focus on Regla and her
sisters Beatrice and Dania, who just
got out of jail for walking home
with a white man after curfew

After Regla, daughter of Africa,
dressed like a bird of paradise from
the singing canopy of the Oriente
jungle, sailed past the old Ballerina,
Alonso, on the ancient steps of the
Gran Teatro de la Habana, where
tourists buy cigars and women
after the evening performance,
the waiter on the terrace at the Hotel
Ingleterra refused to serve her a drink.

Regla is one of the women of Havana
who dress up at night so their children
can eat while their husbands sell black
market cigars and show tourists where
they can buy endangered lobsters in the
barrio chino. I shared my glass of beer with
her while an old grandmother with a baby
slung round her waist and a twelve year old
prostitute whispered to her from their hiding
places between the pots of bougainvillaea,

"Sister, tell the gringa the baby needs medicine."

Regla has never been inside a
grand hotel, it is not allowed,
but she has seen them in movies
and peeked through the windows.
What she remembers is elegant women
with cigarettes and crystal ashtrays.

Regla, named for her saint and baptised
at the church of Santa Regla, a ferry
ride from the district she reigns in gold
earrings and spandex, does not smoke,
even though her relatives, the *torcedores*,
get free cigars from the Partagas
Factory, where they roll tobacco while
someone tells stories and sings to them.

When we call from home on her feast day,
we tell Regla her wish is our command.
She can have dresses and new shoes,
a camera to photograph her child, but
all Regla wants us to send is a glass
ashtray like the ones she sees in movies
and through the windows of grand hotels.

from The Bursting Test

HER SCENT PATCHOULI

In the end, the Italians hated
Mussolini for his politics and
his music. Tonight you came
to bed smelling like his mistress.
I read in a book she wore patchouli
and nearly went to her death
in a silk nightgown Il Duce bought.
Her murderer was catholic too,
and, in the end, let her dress for
daytime, never mind her normal
daytimes were negligees.

They shot her first, so her lover could
watch, and hung her by her slender ankles
before the mothers of dead Italian soldiers
cut her down and pissed on her face.

Even then she smelled of patchouli,
her last night with Benito,
who already had a church blessed wife.

I read he blew out the candles
and came to the straw
bed on the floor of their jailor's room,
bringing their violins.

There was milk for his ulcer and
honey, as if they were honoured
guests, a bride in her nightgown,
the groom with the requisite
sprig of basilica pinned to his shirt.

Benito and Claretta played violin
in the blackout one last time - no
one remembers what - maybe
Mendelssohn, the forbidden Jewish
composer, and went to sleep, the
partisan's Judas milk on their lips.

I smelled her scent, patchouli, tonight.
I hear a swallow beating its frantic
wings in our house, while you
tighten the strings on your mandolin.

When Claretta Petacci hung upside
down, her passionate blood
rushing the wound in her head,
the sky above her full of insects and
airplanes, sounding like Mendelssohn
coming home, one partisan took off his
belt and tied her skirt round her knees.

I have a secret too,
the wild sister inside me.
If I die backwards the way I was
Born the day Claretta and Mussolini
hung upside down like peasant laundry,
if I go out feet first myself, the nightgown
you ironed with perfume over my face,
will you take off your belt and
cover my little mistakes?

from Love in the Rainforest

WRINKLED COLORATURA

In the photo by Man Ray
which the bass player keeps in his
studio, the woman is undressed.
By now, I realize she would be
old, but then she was perfect,
a French twist in her hair, her
naked back lovely and strong.
She is wide in the hips. Her
sound holes look like exquisite
birthmarks. Maybe Man Ray
imagined them, his camera
loving her like a bow, the way
the bass player touches his ancient
appassionata, Miss Amati, the
way he admires her skin and
excellent tone, her girlish pirouette
on one high heel. *E anche vecchia,*
Miss Amati, but she sings better now,

for him.

When he caresses her,
I close my eyes and imagine
naked women all over the world
revealing strings and frets,
flared and resonant thighs, the
low pitched shape of female love.
I think of Man Ray getting old,
his model curling and yellowing
in his hands. I think of you at
night with your ear on my belly,
my wrinkled coloratura sister
singing better than ever for you.

from Love in the Rainforest

Cadenzas

O MAGNIFICAT

When cars filled with boy
sopranos drive themselves
through the holes in ruined
cities singing *O magnificat,*
St. Anselm's proof for the
existence of God; then our
tongues begins to search for the
right words in gaps in our teeth.

The tongue magnifies, our
dentist tell us; in every crack
and crevice a story is hiding,
waiting to come out and frighten
anyone who won't believe
the sum is always greater.

The sum of what, we ask,
greater than what, O *magnificat,*
there are so many voices every
one of them hungry, every
one of them calling for help.

Fill the crack in the earth that
swallowed the leg of the young
ballerina in Sichuan province;
fill the tears in the veil worn by
women stoned to death in Kabul;
fill the empty stomachs of children
starving in the wastelands of Darfur;
fill in the time between gunshots
where children soldier in jungles,
fill the treble holes in the ocean
vacated by singing mammals.

O *magnificat,* it is human to
magnify gaps between molars,
holes in the ozone, caveat in kisses,
and the holy emptiness of longing.
That is why, after all this time,
we are still speaking in tongues.

THE RIVER THAT STILL

She sits by the window watching her
special television, the nurse says; only
today the moving pictures don't move -
not the dark sea in the Selkirk Narrows,
not birds with heads tucked under their
wings, not cars abandoned in snow drifts.
"Do you like snow?" her companion asks
and her social face decomposes for a
moment while her mind searches for the
word and finds only blank pages turning.
There are so many words for water, all
of them buried in the storm. "Sometimes
yes, and sometimes no," she is pleased
with her enigmatic answer. This is how
she learned to navigate the river that still
remembers the words she's forgotten.

She can think back to the day she was born-.
that part is easy - thinks rain, her water symbol,
the life she has led skipping over river rocks,
some of them notes in a tragic aria, even though
the key to music is avoiding the wrong ones.

She sees coloured lights in the blizzard.
What do they mean? It could be the one
she's expecting, not one of the husbands
she found on glass strewn dance floors or
the wailing sirens that carried her to the
hospital for broken hearts, but the mystery,
"sometimes yes, you know." She holds out
her arms to embrace the stillborn note she
hears in the silence of snow, expecting her
angel to step inside; and her angel does,
replacing the mute air with a child, so she
can hold onto the real reason why water
stops moving. It is so the snow can sing,

LAST FERRY FROM KARAKOY

He stands up and, with his hand on his heart
in the Turkish fashion, offers the last seat on
the last ferry from Karakoy to a tourist with
her hair uncovered. What are they thinking,
the beautiful Turkish men, their heads filled
with prayer five times a day and the erotic
deficits of lives neutralized by fear of the
godless world? What is going on behind the
blank stares of women in hajib? In this time,
half way between sunset over Sultanahmet
and the unknown, she doesn't care. A man
stands up, possibly remembering back to the
beginning, and she takes his seat, both of them
daring to imagine a time when her long hair might
have wrapped itself around his body hardened
by sunshine and work in the orange groves.

Now he stands with his hand on his heart
and legs apart as the ferryboat rocks on the
turbulent waters where a great poet once swam
the Bosphorus from Europe to Asia, over the
shipwrecks and drowned sailors, over amphoras
full of olive oil and gold and virgins thrown in
to cheat the Ottoman sultans who came before
tourists. Nothing is said because the man and
women speak different languages and there
are no appropriate words for the last crossing.

FORGETTING WAS YOUNG

My mother is starting to lose the
secrets passed from woman to woman,
stories from before, boats hauled up,
scraping over rocks and barnacles,
hard to walk on, so we felt the cruel
sound of waves breaking in shells
the shape and colour of infant ears.

There was one she buried at the beach,
in a castle decorated with glass, sand in
her white satin shoes, when the world
she is now forgetting was young.

Now her blood feels like sand. The details
of sand move through her, telling the time,
counting the faces that surface in the same
anxious wait as for lost children, who
come up at last from the sea for air.

Last night, in the dark, my mother
went fishing for the man she married
before she discovered the salty
taste of women asleep in the tide.

She couldn't grasp it, her hands
frantic, cupping the water as bodies
swam through the dark, the dead
floating upside down, their faces
void, their voices drowning at sea.

Red sky at night, they say, is a sailor's delight,
but my mother couldn't sleep. Her sheets
smelled like sails. Fish slipped through her net.

Then came the hook, a trumpet voluntary,
something old cast in the brass flourish
of sunrise, wedding cake under her pillow,
silver print on a paper napkin, a child
conceived at sea, the memory surprised
in its sleep, and the note by note silver
egress of fish swimming through grey
layers of dawn, my father's name.

from Muscle Memory

EXCEPT FOR ONE

Yesterday, someone was buried.
Limousines rolled by with their
lights on, tinted windows rolled
up, except for one, open a crack,
wide enough for the hands of
a child, his fingers ecstatic as
puppies riding into the wind.

For twenty years we rode in a
hearse, the windows closed.
We couldn't see out or in, spent
so much time in the dark, now
it is hard to remember your face.

Except in Venice, where the light
was perfect. The children ate ice
cream all afternoon and in the
evening our son, the *piccolo
cantore*, sang in the piazza, filled
his gondolier's hat with coins he
put under his pillow so every time
he moved we could hear it. Tonight
Venice, he said in his sleep, his voice
sounding like money, Italian royalty
arguing in bed, tomorrow the world.

The next day, at the Lido, a hairdresser
put his hand on my breast. *Mi sciocco*,
he said. *Prego, mi scusi.* We had lunch
in the grand hotel and rented a seaside
cabana. I remember making love in the
wooden hut, (Even though you never
did say love),while the children played
in the sand, Italian sunlight slanting

through vents in the swinging door at
the beach where Mahler wrote that
beautiful music, Death in Venice, the
death of our marriage, our children's
hands, thirty fingers in a funeral cortege
fluttering through the louvers.

from The Saning

WEEK-ENDS AT THE BUDDHA HOTEL

The Buddha Hotel we found on the road
to beautiful is filling up now,
with the clay bodies of men.
We are spending week-ends of a thousand
happinesses digging through garden
compost to the dirt at the bottom.

The sound of things changing and remaining
the same could be opera by Wagner,
worms driving their soft bodies
through tunnels of rotting refuse,
everything, everyone singing at once,
holy men waiting to be found in the mud,
the clematis, the raspberries,
an old poet lying there, giving dictation
refusing to go for a last spin
with the angel riding his chest.

On Monday mornings, the garbage men take
the rest of the rubbish away in their truck.
They sit in the cab cracking jokes,
singing along with the radio, some hit
tunes from the time before compost,
while things we refuse to keep
bounce like those balls in old movie
songs over every bump in the road.

Long before seatbelts and road-kill
purses became fashionable, we wondered
what the boys were doing when we were
stealing the keys to our family cars
and driving over speed bumps,
fast as we could, hitting the ceiling
with our heads and the soft leather
seats with the otherwise unexplored
countries our well-travelled mothers

called "down there," while we
closed our eyes and imagined we were out
riding gods we'd been warned about, men
with mysterious bumps in their jeans.

Later, when we found out that boys
closed their eyes and whispered
words like "Ford" and "chassis"
while we were promising "love you forever,"
we knew the bumps in their highways
were the pink bodies of girls
lying on their backs singing songs
the garbage men learned from their fathers.

Now we go for drives every Sunday
over the same concrete obstructions
that make the garbage men laugh
and sing harder, as hard as they can,
because this is the season for digging through
summer and fall, the smell of ripe fruit
and coffee, and making gods out of clay,
where a blue lotus blooms every time
the worms in the compost make love.

We lie with our eyes wide shut,
making love in the dark, trying not to
read the think bubbles exhaled by husbands
when we are riding the garbage truck
like dogs with wind in our faces,
because our minds are palaces
filled with the holy men
we find in the dirt, all of them
shaped like gods, and we love them
hard as we can, over every bump in the road.

from The Bursting Test

HIS BEAUTIFUL PRAYER SHAWL

You smelled it first, near the statue of Buddha
covered in apple blossoms, his beautiful prayer
shawl. We'd buried our faces in the lilies and
narcissus while something moved in the wind,
and you wondered if the wood was possessed.
For days, we circled the tree, the blossoms so
thick on the branches we couldn't see past them.

Let us pray, we said, our life decorated with holy
images: the Mexican crucifix, the Israeli menorah,
the dream catcher, the Buddhist prayer hotel,
which holds in its tiny cubicles the ashes of holy
men mixed with mud. We call this compost,
the sanctified blend of the living and the dead.

The gods and saints have been good. We live
in a first world country with blessed rivers and
sacred mountains. We mix leaves with kitchen
garbage to feed the garden. There is so much
we throw out. Rodents nest in our leftovers.

Did you smell a rat?

Our *papier maché* Santa Regla holds a child
over a fish in the shrine we bought in the
Havana market. *Is it fish we smell,* last week's
garbage wrapped in terrible news? Our First
Nations believe that fish bones should return
to the sea so they may be dressed again.

It is a holy obligation.

We both know what will happen in our chosen
garden. We watched the boy who lives in the
park pick imaginary glass from his face. We saw
him eating from garbage cans. When the cold
weather comes, the beautiful prayer shawl on
Buddha's shoulders will rot, the dead leaves
will fall; and the messenger hanging in the
apple branches will reveal himself again.

from Muscle Memory

THE AESTHETICS OF DYING

I consider the aesthetics of dying. Maybe it hurts less than the struggle to love on a flat world. Maybe it is beautiful and tidy, the disappearance of pain. First I would choose the music. I think I would like something operatic. Tosca running off her parapet or maybe Valkyries riding into the rainforest. Perhaps a Mozart piano concerto. I want to go with a stunning flash. I would like to sit on my silk embroidered chair, explode and vanish, leaving nothing but my silver bracelet and reading glasses— the autoerotic, autopyronic woman, full of lust and igneous food. I think this can happen to women of spirit, who focus celestial light on their very centres, the place a compass would have to penetrate to make a perfect circle, like Giotto putting himself where the lines of the cross intersect. We could stay up all night arguing as to where that place might be, depending on whether a woman was long or short waisted. It is like finding the G spot. Locate the place where fire burns brightest and you will see stars exploding in ordinary furniture.

from The Woman at Mile 0, Love in the Rainforest

MOVING LIKE WATER

It is never the same, but this
time the Zen monk travels light.
He swings his hands from side
to side, rubbing the soft insides
of his arms against his saffron
robes. The redressed holy man
has no elbows. He moves like
water, his begging bowl attached
to his belt, his insect strainer
banging against it, making
the raw percussion of rice.

The monk has experienced the
lives of flies smashed on wind
shields, eaten by carnivores,
strangled in protein filaments
like women who walk over golden
splinters on feet bound in silk.
Last time, he was a transvestite
walking these streets after dark,
and before that a bicycle courier
sandwiched between speeding
cars, and, before living memory,
a shipwreck victim whose skirts
filled with water and pulled him
all the way down the stairs to the
sun at the bottom of the galaxy.

When the monk has picked his
way among everything there to
be seen or stepped on, he will
sit by the road and strain his tea.
He will watch all the things he's
been missing: the wheels going
round, men picking meat from

their teeth, and wind that lifts
summer dresses, exposing the
evening star. He will not swallow
tea leaves, flies, or the dreams
of his fellow travelers. He has
found his vocation. This time
the monk is dressed for moving
like water and touching the idea
of becoming invisible at last.

ACKNOWLEDGEMENTS

The author wishes to thank the editors, publishers, co-authors, broadcasters and illustrators of her work, which includes poetry, fiction, playwriting, journalism, songwriting, performing and illustrating. She is also grateful for her many friends in poetry, for the recognition of national and international awards and for translation of her work. Special thanks to her husband Rick van Krugel and to Ekstasis Editions. The poems in this book were selected with the help and advice of poet, songwriter and editor Carol Ann Sokoloff.

Poems from this collection first appeared in books by the following publishers:

Oolichan Books, *The Woman at Mile Zero*, 1990
Exile Editions, *Love in the Rain Forest*, 1995
Sono Nis Press, *Heaven Cake*, 1997
Sono Nis Press, *The Saning*, 1999
Guernica Editions, *The Bursting Test*, 2002
Médecins Sans Frontieres chapbook, *Take Heart*, 2009
Ekstasis Editions, *Muscle Memory*, 2009
Ekstasis Editions, *Framing the Garden*, 2011

Several of the poems have received awards or prizes:

Voices Israel, Reuben Rose Prize
The Cardiff International Poetry Prize,
The Stephen Leacock Poetry Prize,
Arc Poem of the Year,
The National Poetry Prize,
The Bridport Prize,
The Petra Kenney International Poetry Prize,
The Acorn Rukeyser Award,
and The Montreal International Poetry Prize

The poems in this present collection are selected from eight poetry books, most of which are now out of print, plus new poems. These poetry books and chapbooks were published during the twenty years of living in Victoria, and raising hell, from 1990 to 2012. The poems in *Homing: New & Selected Poems* are ordered for the most part thematically, according to the ideas and concern that compel me to write poetry. The poems in this book have not been substantially altered from their original publications, although a few poems are edited or revised.